Zoom In on Technology Pioneers

Marie Curie

Jennifer Strand

abdopublishing.com

Published by Abdo Zoom™, PO Box 398166, Minneapolis, Minnesota 55439. Copyright © 2017 by Abdo Consulting Group, Inc. International copyrights reserved in all countries. No part of this book may be reproduced in any form without written permission from the publisher. Abdo Zoom™ is a trademark and logo of Abdo Consulting Group, Inc.

Printed in the United States of America, North Mankato, Minnesota
092016
012017

THIS BOOK CONTAINS
RECYCLED MATERIALS

Cover Photo: Everett Historical/Shutterstock Images
Interior Photos: Everett Historical/Shutterstock Images, 1, 10; Ann Ronan Picture Library Heritage Images/ Newscom, 5; iStockphoto, 6–7; Oxford Science Archive Heritage Images/Newscom, 7, 12; AP Images, 8, 13, 16; World History Archive/Newscom, 9; Keystone-France/Gamma-Rapho/Getty Images, 14–15; The Print Collector Heritage Images/Newscom, 17; Everett - Art/Shutterstock Images, 18; Gawrav Sinha/ iStockphoto, 19

Editor: Brienna Rossiter
Series Designer: Madeline Berger
Art Direction: Dorothy Toth

Publisher's Cataloging-in-Publication Data
Names: Strand, Jennifer, author.
Title: Marie Curie / by Jennifer Strand.
Description: Minneapolis, MN : Abdo Zoom, 2017. | Series: Technology pioneers
    | Includes bibliographical references and index.
Identifiers: LCCN 2016948683 | ISBN 9781680799255 (lib. bdg.) |
    ISBN 9781624025112 (ebook) | 9781624025679 (Read-to-me ebook)
Subjects: LCSH: Curie, Marie, 1867-1934--Juvenile literature. | Chemists--
    Poland--Biography--Juvenile literature. | Women chemists--Poland--
    Biography--Juvenile literature. | Chemists--France--Biography--Juvenile
    literature. | Women chemists--France--Juvenile literature.
Classification: DDC 540.92 [B]--dc23
LC record available at http://lccn.loc.gov/2016948683

Table of Contents

Introduction

Marie Curie was a scientist.
She studied **X-rays**. She was the
first woman to win a **Nobel Prize**.

Early Life

Marie was born on November 7, 1867. She lived in Poland.

She loved to study
math and science.

8

Marie married Pierre Curie.
He was a scientist, too.

They worked together.
They studied X-rays. They also
discovered two new **elements**.

In 1903 the Curies won a Nobel Prize for **physics.**

No woman had won
this prize before.

Pierre died in 1906. Marie kept working.

She did many **experiments**.
She learned about the
new elements.

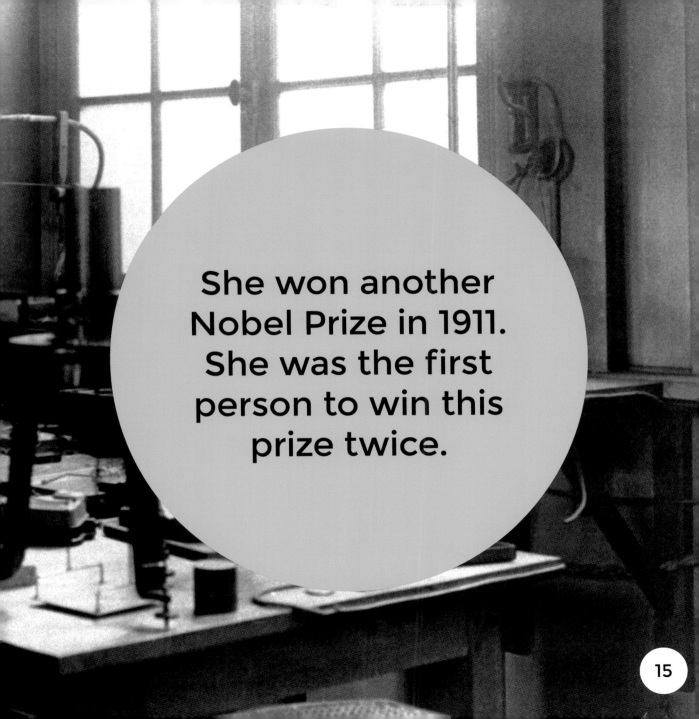

She won another Nobel Prize in 1911. She was the first person to win this prize twice.

Legacy

People did not yet know X-rays were dangerous. Curie's work with them made her sick.

She died on July 4, 1934.

Curie's work was very important. She helped people learn about X-rays.

Many doctors
use X-rays today.

Marie Curie

Born: November 7, 1867

Birthplace: Warsaw, Poland

Husband: Pierre Curie

Known For: Curie was a famous scientist. She studied X-rays.

Died: July 4, 1934

Key Dates

1867: Maria Salomea Sklodowska is born on November 7.

1895: Marie and Pierre Curie marry.

1898: Marie and Pierre Curie announce their discovery of new elements.

1903: Marie and Pierre Curie win the Nobel Prize in Physics.

1911: Marie Curie wins the Nobel Prize in Chemistry.

1934: Curie dies on July 4.

Glossary

element - one of the substances from which all matter is composed.

experiment - a scientific test.

Nobel Prize - an important award given out each year.

physics - the science that deals with matter, energy, motion, and force.

X-rays - invisible beams of light that can go through solid objects.

Booklinks

For more information
on **Marie Curie**, please visit
booklinks.abdopublishing.com

Zoom In on Biographies!

Learn even more with the Abdo Zoom
Biographies database. Check out
abdozoom.com for more information.

Index